fast
thinking:
discipline

D0526305

PEARSON EDUCATION LIMITED

Head Office:
Edinburgh Gate
Harlow CM20 2JE
Tel: +44 (0)1279 623623
Fax: +44 (0)1279 431059

London Office:
128 Long Acre
London WC2E 9AN
Tel: +44 (0)20 7447 2000
Fax: +44 (0)20 7240 5771
Website: www.business-minds.com

———————————————

First published in Great Britain in 2001

ISBN 0 273 65318 0

British Library Cataloguing in Publication Data
A CIP catalogue record for this book can be obtained from the British Library

10 9 8 7 6 5 4 3 2 1

Typeset by Pantek Arts Ltd, Maidstone, Kent.
Printed and bound in Great Britain by Ashford Colour Press, Hampshire

The Publishers' policy is to use paper manufactured from sustainable forests.

fast
thinking:
discipline

▶ **choose the right procedure**

▶ **interview with confidence**

▶ **resolve the situation**

by Richard Templar

contents

introduction

So, things have got worse and you haven't taken action in time. Or maybe this matter's been dumped on your desk and you have to deal with it without knowing what it is all about. And now it's come to a discipline interview that has been pencilled in for tomorrow. The clock's ticking and you haven't really thought about what procedure you've got to adopt, what you are going to say, how you are going to handle this one if it gets difficult, what happens if you don't put in place some follow-up procedure to make sure it doesn't happen again – and you've got to do all this with diplomacy and restraint. And show the other members of your team that you are on top of your job, treat them all fairly and yet won't stand for any nonsense. Seems like a pretty tall order.

Here's the guide to help you through it with ease and expertise, and have you looking good at the end of it.

Now, we all know that time is our enemy – there simply isn't enough of it to go round – so what you have to do is cut out the irrelevant and work only with the necessary stuff. That's what this book will enable you to do. It will tell you how to handle a discipline interview clearly and precisely without any waffle or boring bits. It will show you what you have to do when the discipline interview is only a day away. And there is even a section for the discipline interview in an hour's time and one for taking disciplinary action in 15 minutes.

This book will also guide you through the process of handling ongoing discipline concerns, how to handle difficult people, how to be assertive yourself so you feel confident and comfortable administering discipline, and what to do in a real discipline crisis.

Sure, it's always better to have more time, but we live in the real world and we have to work with what we've got. There's no time to lose so what you want is:

 tips for looking as if you are handling this confidently when you know you're really quaking in your boots

 shortcuts to speed the process up

 checklists to run through so you make sure you've forgotten nothing

Sure, it's always better to have more time, but we live in the real world and we have to work with what we've got

... and all put together clearly and simply. And short enough to read fast of course.

Let's assume you've got a day to prepare for this discipline interview. Ideally you would have had longer, but events have overtaken you and you've simply no room for manoeuvre or delay. You've got to prepare at the speed of life – so take the phone off the hook, make a quick coffee, and settle back to read fast.

HANDLING DISCIPLINE AT THE SPEED OF LIFE

This book is going to get you through the five key stages of handling discipline:

1 The first thing to do is identify your objective so you know exactly what is required of you.

2 After this comes taking immediate action – what to do on a daily basis for dealing with minor problems of discipline.

3 The discipline interview itself – when all other forms of treatment have failed and you have to take serious steps – includes collecting the relevant information, handling the interview itself, and using your company's codes of practice and procedures. And, of course, we'll look at the most difficult of all discipline interviews – the termination of employment interview.

4 Handling difficult interviews: what to do and how to react when people respond in a less than helpful way, and how to remain calm and handle the situation effectively and diplomatically.

5 Lastly we'll look at what happens when it's not a discipline matter at all but really a counselling interview you may need to be holding – when you can't really take disciplinary action because the case is a much more sensitive issue.

The first thing to do is identify your objective so you know exactly what is required of you.

fast thinking
gambles

Of course we would all like more time but the fact remains – you've got to handle this discipline interview tomorrow. Ideally you would have had more time to prepare if only that had been possible. Fast thinking will stop you making horrendous mistakes and will achieve your objective comfortably. So what's the point of allowing more time if we can wing it effectively this time? Well, no matter how well you handle this, there are risks, and when your time is limited your options are also limited.

So what's the downside of preparing a discipline interview at the last minute rather than taking more time? Well …

▸ **You may not have carried out sufficient research thus leaving yourself wide open to charges of unfairness or just plain being wrong – and you won't have time to make sure of all the facts.**

▸ **You may jump in at the deep end and react badly yourself if cornered by a difficult interviewee.**

- You may not have carried out your company's discipline code of practice as well or as correctly as necessary – and that could lead to the dreaded tribunal.

- In your haste you might overlook some essential aspect of the matter that might indicate it is more of a counselling concern than a discipline interview – and hence risk upsetting people more than you need.

- You may be tempted to handle a termination of employment interview yourself without having time to seek the relevant legal advice – and again that leads to the dreaded tribunal.

Fast thinking will enable you to handle this situation with care and tact as well as looking good and being seen to be fair – but for a truly magnificent display of team leadership qualities, do try and leave a bit more time next time. Of course, with any discipline matter you need to take decisive and effective action as quickly as possible to nip things in the bud but that should be done on a day-to-day basis as we will see shortly. A discipline interview, on the other hand, needs time to think about, prepare for and plan it. No good rushing these things even if you are at the cutting edge of management. We need to think fast but think effectively. Next time leave more time. But for this time we'll get you through it and have you come up smelling of roses and without leaving a trail of debris behind you.

1 your objective

One of the first things we usually do in a crisis is panic. We stop thinking about our long-term goals and how to manage effectively, and simply seek ways to get us through this quickly. Quick can sometimes be deadly, as well as slower than if we take a little time out to catch our breath and consider the best plan of action. Discipline interviews – and indeed any aspect of discipline – is fraught with danger. You are dealing with people here, and in their most vulnerable state – when they are on the defensive. It is a minefield of emotional pitfalls and potential outbursts. No one likes being disciplined – in fact no one likes doing the disciplining but it has to be done. And you owe it to your team to be as calm and effective as possible.

This means sitting down and thinking clearly about what you are doing. Yes, it means setting an objective. What are you trying to achieve? Easy to say 'Give old Bill a good roasting for being late so often,' but is that really what you want to achieve? What happens in the long term? You might well have expressed your anger at Bill, got something out of your system and ended up feeling better, but what about Bill? Have you encouraged him to turn up on time? Found out why he is late so often? Made it plain to the rest of your team that you care about them? Been seen to deal with discipline matters fairly and calmly? I think not.

Let's have a rethink about this. You need to work through the three key stages of discipline in order to set an objective:

1 Find out why – clarify the facts.
2 Take appropriate action – action that deals with the situation as and when it occurs without damaging morale amongst the other team members.
3 Make sure it isn't an ongoing problem – set up procedures to monitor it long term and to make sure it doesn't recur.

So, if old Bill is late on a regular basis you need to find out why – and why it hasn't been dealt with previously; decide on suitable action – this may not be a discipline interview matter at all but a quiet word on the side instead; then put in place systems to monitor it and correct it and prevent it occurring again as far as possible.

Thus your objective becomes a lot clearer: to establish the truth, to deal appropriately with it, and to make sure it doesn't happen again. That's better than just sounding off at Bill and getting his back up – as well as the rest of the team's backs.

Now you've identified your objective write it down. Spend five minutes thinking about it. This is your mission statement for dealing with all discipline matters in the future.

thinking smart

If you spend five minutes thinking about your objective you actually can create more time in the future. If you get it right now, you won't have to waste time attending a tribunal or dealing with potentially damaging litigation or simply rebuilding your team's morale. If you think five minutes is too much to spare, consider the implications of not thinking about your objective.

for next time

Set your objective earlier. That's it. And now you've done it this time you won't have to do it next time – it should always remain the same for all discipline matters.

This is your mission statement for dealing with all discipline matters in the future

2 taking immediate action

So, we've got to move on quickly now as the clock is still our worst enemy and we are thinking – and working – at the speed of life. Let's get cracking.

Administering discipline tends to take one of three approaches. There is the instant discipline, where you see someone doing something wrong and you correct it on the spot – the equivalent to a cuff round the ear.

There is the slightly more serious offence that requires pulling the person to one side and privately having a word – a sort of kick up the back side.

And then there is the more serious matter that requires a formal discipline interview (which we will look at in the next chapter) – the equivalent to six of the best.

Obviously the administering of any punishment never takes a physical form and these examples are just there to emphasize a point: please don't really hit your staff.

Each of these three requires a slightly different approach. Let's look at the first two. Both of these are for less serious infringements of company procedures, but they do need to be handled a little differently.

THE CUFF ROUND THE EAR

You have a team member that you catch coming in late – what are you going to do? Well, firstly think back to when you've come in late. How did you feel when you were ticked off? In fact, how did you feel being ticked off for any mistake that you made unintentionally and that you never really saw coming? Sure, it makes you feel resentful. The person telling you off obviously doesn't have a clue how you feel, whether or not you are genuinely sorry, what their treatment of you is doing, or indeed what effect it will have on your future performance or behaviour. This 'ticking off' might clear their congestion but it certainly doesn't do any good for morale, does it? And we saw earlier that maintaining morale was part of our objective. So what are you going to do knowing now that such a ticking off can be detrimental?

Well, the cuff round the ear might have worked way back when small boys went scrumping and got caught, but in this modern world of team leadership we cannot afford to rile people, put their backs up, or be caught on the hop. We have to handle situations sensitively and diplomatically – and fairly of course. If Bill has been in late twice this week and you take action, be pretty sure that when Katie was late twice in the same week last month you followed exactly the same procedure. Don't haul Bill over the coals when you let Katie off. Likewise don't let Bill off if you gave Katie a hard time, she will remember her treatment and if you let Bill off she will be resentful.

So, be consistent at all times. Be fair and as just as you can. Now I know you might not like having to confront team members who are slipping, but confront them you must. Team leadership qualities involve being assertive and being prepared to be out there in the firing line to get the best from your team. If you let this go, it will get worse and the rest of the team will suffer. You have to nip things in the bud or they will bloom in an altogether unfortunate way. It is your job to maintain good order and discipline.

thfhkthinking smart

KEEP RECORDS

Maintain some system of your own whereby you keep a record of your tolerance levels. If you accept that a team member can be late once a month without you saying anything then write that down on a card for your own private use. If you catch someone smoking in a no-smoking zone what action do you take? – write it down. Try to run through all breaches of discipline you've encountered in the last six months and make a note of what you did. This tolerance level record will serve you well as you can then treat the staff fairly and they will expect you to do so. And it's very quick just to pull out a card before you storm off and steam in and jump the gun; it gives you a slight breathing space and allows you to see what you did before when you weren't having such a bad day.

So what are you going to say?

Remember your objective – *find out the truth.* Don't tell Bill anything – ask him instead. Give Bill a chance to explain. He may have a good reason. He may have cleared his lateness with another manager or team leader who has inadvertently forgotten to tell you, or he may well be aware that he is late and he is now feeling pretty rotten about it. Charging in and telling him off also tells him you think little of him and that you don't care if he becomes demoralized. So always:

- Find out the circumstances first.
- Give the team member a chance to explain.
- Accept their apology if it is offered in good grace.
- Respect their feelings about the matter and don't give them a hard time.
- Give them a chance to make amends.

There, that didn't hurt too much, did it? And you didn't have to cuff anyone round the ear.

Point out to Bill he is late by all means but give him the chance to explain. Accept his apology and he might well say, 'sorry, the car broke down but I'll make sure it doesn't happen again. I'm getting a new battery tonight so this shouldn't be a problem again.'

End on a positive upbeat note. Pat Bill on the back and tell him it happens to us all from time to time. This is a first infringement so you don't want to make too big a thing of it. If Bill's car breaks down every Friday morning you will have to go to plan B – the kick up the backside, which we will look at in a moment.

WE ARE ALL HUMAN

Don't expect too much of people and they will surprise you. If you allow them to be human they will occasionally foul up, let you down, run amok, slope off, be naughty, make mistakes, and generally behave as humans do. And you will be expecting it and not be surprised. What you might be surprised by is how infrequently they do so. If you expect them to be perfect you have only disappointment waiting for you – and you will be surprised how often you are disappointed.

But have we finished?

Not quite. There a few more rules to stick to:

▸ **Never criticize a team member in front of anyone else.**

▸ **Deal with things as and when they happen rather than letting them fester.**

▸ **Be very sure of your facts before diving in.**

▸ **Make sure the person understands the implications of their actions.**

GENUINE MISTAKES

The overwhelming majority of mistakes in any organization happen by accident. They are exactly that – accidents. Treat them as such. If the person making the mistake realizes what they have done and regrets it, your job is virtually done for you. There is then absolutely no point in giving them a hard time – they know what they have done and regret it. What more can you do to improve that situation? Make sure they understand how it happened and that they have learnt from it. Be magnanimous enough to thank them for owning up to their mistake – good one this as they'll be happy to tell you next time they foul up and not try to conceal anything.

Never criticize a team member in front of anyone else

This really is an unbreakable rule. You must be aware that bawling people out in front of their colleagues is unacceptable. It does nothing for their morale and certainly embarrasses the others. If you follow the rules of good discipline management outlined just now, you will realize that bawling anyone out is unproductive. All you have to do is pull them to one side – 'Bill, can I have a quick word?' – and you move to a corridor or out of earshot. Easy.

Deal with things as and when they happen

If you see someone coming in late, don't put it off until after your mid-morning coffee or later in the week. Talk to them there and then. Catch them before they've got their coat off, but do it nicely. Ask; remember, don't yell or tell. You can even be light-heartedly kind about it, 'So, Katie, get caught in the Tube strike? Well, you voted for him.' Don't be sarcastic or micky-taking, but you can be friendly. Obviously the friendliness evaporates if this is a habitual problem, but that is another matter. Nipping it in the bud should be your mission statement for dealing with infrequent minor lapses of discipline.

Be sure of the facts

But is Katie late? Are you sure? Has she pencilled in a dentist appointment since you last looked at the diary? Did she clear this with someone else? Has she been out on company business since arriving at work before you? Was she caught in idle chit-chat with the MD in the lift and couldn't get away? Was she out in another department organizing a whip round for your birthday present? (This actually happened to me many years ago when I was relatively inexperienced as a general manager of a large organization and, boy, did I feel dumb and embarrassed.) Do you have a good system of checking in so you can monitor lateness? Perhaps Katie is only taking advantage of sloppy time-keeping rituals that have gone on unnoticed for quite a while, until you noticed her this morning, that is. It happens sometimes that someone gets caught for an offence that everyone else is also committing but the team leader hasn't noticed. It is then very unfair to punish or blame anyone except yourself for poor systems. We'll look at implementing company codes of practice a little later. So make sure of your facts before taking action. And sometimes, the only way to make sure of your facts is to say something – ask if you're not sure. You can't be blamed for that just so long as you are asking and not accusing.

Make sure they understand the implications of their actions

If Bill is late, it means Harry can't finish the paper work, and Sue can't take the stock sheets over to Brenda, who then can't process them in time for the internal audit due this afternoon which means the rest of the team will be let down – that sort of thing. Emphasize the fact that you are a team and if one team member is not pulling their weight or taking their responsibilities seriously it undermines the whole shooting match. Don't make too big a thing of it for minor infractions, but it is worth pointing out how dependent on them you are – this makes them feel they are letting *you* down if they foul up rather than just themselves.

MAINTAINING DISCIPLINE

No one likes to be told off and no one likes to do the telling off. And if you maintain good discipline there is no need for either. Set standards yourself of course – don't be late or take home free pens if you don't expect the team to do so. But there will always be times when someone somewhere likes to take advantage. This then becomes the kick up the backside. Reserve it for persistent infringements. It is the informal discipline chat. It isn't a full-blown discipline interview which deals with major incidents, but rather a chance to try and put things right before they get really bad. The informal chat is for persistent infringements of minor company policy – habitual lateness rather than being drunk on duty, occasional sloppiness in work standards rather than serious misconduct, such as being caught having sex in the store room, persistent parking in the MD's parking space rather than writing off a company car showing off in the car park. That sort of thing.

The kick up the backside

One of the key rules for the informal chat is to catch it early. This isn't quite nipping it in the bud. You may have tried the ear cuffing technique and it failed. Now you have to move on to a more serious technique – the kick up the backside. Sometimes it is all someone needs to pull them back into line. Suppose Katie was late once and you had a quiet word. This had an effect at the time but now she is late almost every day. You can't let it go on. Once it has happened four or five times, you have to have the informal chat. If you let it go on for months, there is an implied agreement to her actions – she expects to come in late because you haven't said anything.

Tightening up their performance

At this stage you are still dealing with a fairly minor problem, so there is no need for any official action, such as written warnings. You don't have to get het up about it as you are dealing with it. All you are doing is tightening up the person's performance to get the very best from them. It isn't a major issue yet. If you announce it as a matter for a major disciplinary interview you've overreacted. Basically the informal chat takes place before you even need to issue a verbal warning – which you always do in writing of course to protect both yourself and the team member.

Rules

The rules for an informal chat are quite similar to those of the informal cuff round the ear:

▸ **Always go somewhere private** – this is between you and the team member and there is no need for anyone else to know what is being said – or that you are even having this chat.

▸ **Be pretty damned sure of the facts** before calling someone in for an informal chat – you'll end up with egg on your face if you are wrong.

▸ **Be consistent** – you might think that you are being so, but make a record and check back that you always handle this particular problem in the same way.

▸ **Give the person a chance to have their say** – there may be more going on than you realize, or they may already feel pretty bad about the situation and don't need you sounding off to add to their troubles. Let them express their regret and offer solutions before you play the heavy-handed card.

▸ **Focus on the problem not the person** – it is their behaviour that is at fault, not them.

▸ **Make it short and sweet** – you are there to discuss this particular problem, not their entire career or anyone else's. Stick to the facts and don't go round the houses or get sidetracked by any other issues. Be assertive but fair, be succinct and brief.

▸ **End on a positive note** – no matter how you feel about the problem or the person, always end on an upbeat tone so they go away feeling good about themselves, you and the informal chat. Don't finish on a sour note whatever you do, as the ramifications can be long term and disastrous.

THE NAUGHTY CHILD

If you have a naughty child at home and constantly tell them that they are naughty, you are reinforcing the problem not solving it. If you tell them they are a good child who has done a naughty thing, then you are blaming their behaviour and not them. They are a good child who has done a naughty thing, not a naughty child. This works for team members as well. They are good team members who have done a naughty thing, not bad team members.

Handling the informal chat

So, those are the rules but how do you handle the chat? Easy. Pop your head round the corner of the person's office or workplace and just say, 'Ah, Katie, can I have a quick word with you in my office in five minutes. Thanks.'

Then get them sitting down and remember, don't accuse, ask instead. 'Now, this lateness problem seems to be getting a bit out of hand so I thought you might like a chance to say how you feel we could resolve it. Got any ideas?'

Get them to do all the hard work

Katie is then not being bawled out or told off but given the chance to express herself, outline any problems connected with this matter, and have her say. You aren't being angry or irritated. You are a team leader trying to do what is right for the whole team. You can always point this out. You have a team member who isn't pulling in quite the right direction. That's all you want to accomplish. Get Katie to offer solutions. Get Katie to do all the hard work. That way she will feel part of the discipline process rather than like a small child being told off by her teacher at nursery school.

A lot of managers and team leaders do rather see their role as a parent or teacher when it plainly isn't. Your role is to motivate and encourage, lead and coordinate, inspire and direct. It isn't to tell anyone off or shout at anyone. You are a leader, a director, a guide; not a teacher, parent or police officer.

thinking smart

TAKING RESPONSIBILITY

For every breach of discipline by one of your team members, deduct five points from your own score. If they foul up, you can only blame yourself. Your job is to motivate and inspire them. If they wander off course, you must blame the guide not the porter. You are the guide. You must take responsibility. If they foul up, you must look at your own leadership qualities to see where you have gone wrong.

So, now you know what to say and how to say it all that remains is to call them in and get it over with. Take a deep breath and remember this is part of your job. I know you don't like it – no one does – but see it as an opportunity to rise to a challenge, a chance to improve your own experience and expertise, and a golden opportunity to do it better than all the times it was done badly to you in the past. The cycle of being told off then feeling resentful has to end somewhere. Make sure it is you that ends it – better management today by better methods and better people to inspire a better output. What could be better?

◀ for next time

Keep records of what you did so you can maintain a consistent track record thus keeping the team members sweet and demonstrating your fairness.

Practise different ways of asking what the hell someone thinks they are doing coming in late or whatever without letting them know you are upset, riled or irritated. Make enquiries rather than demanding explanations. Ask open questions (ones that can't be answered with a simple yes or no – more about this later) so you elicit a response. Once you've got them talking, they will quite naturally and without prompting offer an apology and even suggestions as to how to stop it happening again.

Practise treating your team members like grown-ups and see if it doesn't generate a better response from them. Give them the space to be human.

Better management today by better methods and better people to inspire a better output

3 the discipline interview

Quickly now, the clock is still ticking and you've got this discipline interview tomorrow – or in an hour if you're unlucky (see page 90) or even in 15 minutes if you've really drawn the short straw (see page 94). But not so quickly that you don't read this section carefully and take it all in. You are dealing here with a situation fraught with emotional fireworks and charged with sensitive dynamite. Tread softly for you tread on people's feelings, hurts, vulnerabilities and defensiveness. But you still have to enforce company procedure and policy and be an effective team leader. Maintaining good discipline is part of your job – this is what you signed up for.

Now before you go into this interview tomorrow there are five key areas you should have checked thoroughly so you aren't caught on the hop. Make sure that:

- This really is a clear breach of company policy.

- The company policy is clearly understood by each and every member of your team and that they know they have broken the rules.

- This offence is a major one and warrants a discipline interview and not just a cuff round the ear or a kick up the backside – that this really is one for six of the best.

- This offence warrants a discipline interview and is not so serious that the only outcome could be a termination of employment.

- You've got the right person and that they did do it – whatever 'it' is. Make sure of your facts very, very carefully before going down this route.

We'll quickly run through these so your checklist is in place and ticked off before tomorrow.

CLEAR BREACH OF POLICY

Is the offence a clear breach of company policy? There are two parts to any company policy – the written and the unwritten.

Written company policy

The written is what constitutes part of everyone's contract and usually states their working hours and duties, what the company expects from them, and what their job entails. Make sure this is all up to date. You can't bawl someone out for failing to carry out a task if that task isn't and never was part of their job description. They may have been expected to do it but if it ain't written down then they've got you and you have no defence. Make sure that the written part of company policy is kept up to date. Make sure it says what time they are expected to be at work – that sort of thing.

Unwritten company policy

The unwritten part is the sort of normal behaviour you'd expect of anyone – not being drunk on duty, being civil, not taking part in any sexual harassment, being honest, being trustworthy – that sort of stuff. If

CHANGE THE LOCATION

You don't have to hold the interview in your office or a meeting room. Why not have it over lunch rather than just after lunch, or even in the team member's office. Changing the location to a somewhat unorthodox and unexpected one can change the attitude that such meetings can produce. You are there to be the good shepherd, not the parent, so you can be as inventive as you like, just so long as you get the job done with the minimum of resentment or tears.

you catch anyone breaking an unwritten part of company policy think very carefully before bawling them out as you may have found a legal loophole that they might exploit – but do it if you have to. Make sure a record of it is kept and make sure the powers that be are told in order to protect both you and the team member. It might also be worthwhile suggesting that it be included as part of the written company policy.

IS COMPANY POLICY UNDERSTOOD?

Make sure the company policy – written and unwritten – is clearly understood. When inducting a new member of staff (see *Fast Thinking: New Beginner*) it is worth pointing out a subtle clause such as 'and of course we expect you to behave in a responsible and mature way when at work'. This covers you in the eventuality of them fouling up. They can't come back with 'but I never knew I wasn't supposed to be drunk on duty.'

Make sure they fully understand that they have broken the rules. There's not a lot of point in having a discipline interview – which is there, of course, to put things right, not to be a form of telling off sitting down – if they don't understand what they have done wrong or that it was wrong. They must be aware that their conduct was a serious breach of company policy.

IS THIS A MAJOR OFFENCE?

Some managers seem to think that having a discipline interview is a matter for routine and you should have one for any minor infringement of the rules. Others never have one if they can help it. Either extreme is just that – extreme. You hold a discipline interview as and when you need to: not for minor offences and not to be avoided at all costs. Every team leader will encounter behaviour that warrants a discipline interview – presumably you have recently, or you wouldn't be holding this interview tomorrow – and should be aware that they are not to be treated lightly, nor are they for minor violations of rules. Reserve the discipline interview for the big stuff.

thinking smart

INVITE A FRIEND

Offer the person the opportunity to bring along a friend if they want. This could be a work colleague or their direct supervisor or a union representative. You have nothing to hide and it reassures them that you are not about to fire them or shout at them or bring up anything personal or anything they aren't prepared for.

DOES THE OFFENCE WARRANT TERMINATION OF EMPLOYMENT?

Some offences are so serious that the only outcome is termination of employment. These matters are certainly not for the discipline interview, although you may have to hold a form of one to:

▶ **establish the truth**

▶ **make the team member aware of the seriousness of their behaviour**

▶ **discuss possible options such as their resignation before you terminate anyway, or a transfer to your Outer Hebrides branch, or a written apology and repayment of all the money – that sort of thing.**

thinking smart

CHOOSE YOUR TIME CAREFULLY

You may not have realized that there are 'good' and 'bad' times to hold discipline interviews. The good time is just after lunch – we are all a bit more mellow when we've just been fed. The bad times are the high-stress times – between 9 and 11 in the morning and between 3 and 5 in the afternoon. In the morning, there is work to be done and an anxious need to be getting on with it. In the afternoon, there is a winding down and thoughts of going home. Best stick to just after lunch.

If the offence warrants a discipline interview, it has to be pretty serious anyway, but not so serious that you need to take advice or seek counsel from a higher authority.

CHECK YOU HAVE THE RIGHT PERSON

It does happens that an offence occurs, you think you've got the person who did it, you hold the interview, only to find out it wasn't them. This leaves you feeling and looking pretty foolish. Make very sure of your facts before launching into this. Establish:

▸ **who did what**

▸ **when it was done**

▸ **how and why it was done – as far as possible**

▸ **who was responsible – this is different from who did it, they may have been acting under someone else's instructions about which you know nothing**

▸ **what has happened since it was done – they may have made efforts to make amends**

▸ **what the ramifications of what they did are – they may use the excuse or defence of 'Well, what does it matter anyway, nothing disastrous has happened'**

▸ **any previous convictions – you need to find out if this is habitual. Have they been transferred from another department because of this sort of behaviour? Is it likely to recur? Are they the only one doing it? Have any other team leaders had any experience of dealing with this issue?**

Whew. That's your checklist pretty well covered. That's what you need to do in advance. Seems a lot but it might take only a few minutes. If you are sure that you've got the right person, and that the offence has been committed, you're almost there. If you aren't sure at any step along the way then reschedule the interview. Don't go in half sure or even three-quarters sure. Be very, very sure, or postpone until you are.

ADVANCE NOTICE

OK, let's jump ahead to tomorrow. What preparations have you made? None? Well, you do need to make some. The team member needs to be told in advance that a discipline interview is scheduled – it's unfair to spring it on them at the last minute. You can't just march them to your office and begin a discipline interview without giving them the chance to marshal their forces and collect their breath as well. They may need to seek union advice, consult a friend, talk to anyone else involved, reschedule any important meetings of their own, or gather any relevant evidence they may have in their defence. I know this isn't a trial but they must be given a full opportunity to 'put their case' so to speak. So give them due warning. Make it a formal interview and set a time and a date

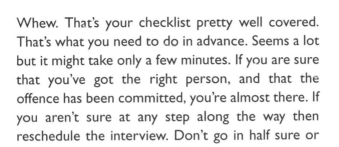

THE PRAISE SANDWICH

We all hate discipline interviews from either side, and when we are the one holding the interview there is always a terrible need to start by giving praise to soften the blow of what is to come. This doesn't work. The person knows what is coming and can see through this technique. They also know you'll end on an upbeat note – some more praise. So the bad news gets sandwiched in between. Instead, begin by saying 'We'll discuss this problem area first then move on to a couple of points I'd like to make about your good progress in X.'

That way they know there is something good to come and you've removed the bread but left the filling – which is what they have come for. It also speeds up the entire process, which is good news for you.

well in advance. I presume you have done this for your discipline interview tomorrow? If not, do it now. Quickly, while there is still time. If you can't, then reschedule the interview.

WHERE TO HOLD THE INTERVIEW

Yes, you can hold it in your own office but there are risks involved. You are subject to endless interruptions. You gain an unfair edge by holding it on your territory – remember this isn't a trial or a battle of wits. You want this team member back on the case and anything you do to help this along will be recognized and respected. Hold the interview, if you can, on neutral territory. Book a meeting room if your company has them. Borrow an office. Use a quiet room where you won't be disturbed. Make sure everyone knows you are out of contact for a specified time – usually half an hour should be sufficient at the most. No one wants these things to go on a second longer than necessary.

Seating

Traditionally, the boss sat behind the big desk and the employee stood in front of it and was duly rollicked for some misdemeanour. That practice has long since died out – and quite rightly so: it was unproductive, seriously undermined morale, and made the employee defensive and hostile. Nowadays we treat people with a lot more respect. Choose the sort of seating arrangement that reflects this. Sitting behind a desk sets up a whole string of assumptions, all of which you need to get rid of. You are not there to instil fear or to intimidate. You are there to nudge a fellow team member kindly back on track. This isn't a difficult process, but it is demanding. You have to tread warily. You are dealing with human beings with real feelings. Sit opposite them by all means, but get rid of the desk. Two chairs brought out to the same side of the desk works well. Sitting in low, comfortable armchairs doesn't seem to work well, as you both sink into an unwork-like relaxation. You need to be alert, professional and businesslike.

So, you've got the room and the seating right. You've got your checklist and obviously the employee's personnel file. You are ready to begin the real job of carrying out the discipline interview.

WRITE IT DOWN

When we begin a discipline interview, there is often a tendency to have a somewhat confrontational eye-to-eye contact. You begin by outlining the problem verbally while the person stares at you. This isn't a good technique as it makes it uncomfortable for both of you. A better way is to hand them a piece of paper with a brief outline of why they are here. They are then obliged to read it – and thus break eye contact – and then you can ask them for their views. You have removed the initial confrontation, which makes life easier and the interview quicker and slicker. It also gives the person a chance to look away from you while receiving the bad news, giving them a greater feeling of control.

THE DISCIPLINE INTERVIEW

How are you going to begin? Let's try a few examples, which are all taken from real interviews:

> 'You're here because I'm bloody well fed up with your constant lateness.'

> 'You knew this was coming. You knew you were pushing your luck, didn't you?'

> 'This is a really serious matter and I don't know whether to bawl you out or fire you.'

> 'I knew when I took you on you'd let me down.'

> 'Let's cut the ****. You're useless at your job and if you don't pull your socks up, you're out.'

All real. All true. All unproductive and unhelpful. These openers do nothing to raise morale. They don't inspire or motivate. They immediately set the team member on the defensive and don't give them any room to explain themselves, make amends, seek new ways to improve, or even make them feel part of a team. They are old-fashioned and out-dated.

Let's see if we can't improve on these openers drawn from the age of the dinosaurs. Never begin with a statement such as:

> 'I expect you know what all this is about.'

> 'This is a discipline interview to discuss your behaviour last Wednesday at the conference.'

'You knew you were breaking company security procedures.'

Begin instead with a simple question. such as:

'Do you know what this is about?'

'So, what happened last Wednesday at the conference?'

'Are you aware that you have breached company security procedures?'

This sets the tone for the whole interview. It is going to be a full and frank discussion. It is not going to be a trial or an interrogation. You are there to set the person back on track. You are not there to administer punishment or haul them over the coals. You are not their parent. If you insist on being a relative, be an avuncular uncle or aunt — kindly and well meaning, friendly and forgiving. I know this might sound as if it goes against the grain of a discipline interview, but you really must ask yourself what you want out of this interview. Is it:

- a confession?
- tears and guilty regrets?
- to find a suitable punishment?
- to make them feel really, really sorry?
- to extract a promise from them never to do it again?

- to make them realize that you are in charge and they must do as you say?
- to make them feel bad about themselves?
- to make them feel bad about the team?
- to make them want to leave?

No, of course not. It is none of these. So what is it? It is to bring them back on track.

That's it. Nothing else. You don't have to make them feel anything – they'll feel it for themselves. You don't have to extract a confession. This is a simple matter of finding out what happened and why and to ensure they are clear about what they did and why it shouldn't have been done. There are no threats, no intimidations, no punishments.

See yourself as a shepherd. One of your flock has strayed and you bring them back into the field. You wouldn't beat a lamb so don't beat a team member. Reassure them, comfort them, explain kindly the error of their ways and bring them back on track.

 thinking smart

GIVE THANKS

Make sure you make a point of thanking the team member for attending. You know they are obliged to – and so do they – but thank them anyway. This is polite and respectful and they will appreciate it. It also lightens the mood of what may be a difficult half an hour for both of you.

Have a quick tot up of how much it costs to recruit staff, train them and employ them and see if being a shepherd rather than a wrathful god of vengeance doesn't make more economic sense.

AFTER THE OPENER

Once you've outlined in the form of a question why the discipline interview is taking place you need to get the person to talk. You won't do this by asking closed questions (ones that require a one-word answer, such as yes or no). You need to ask open questions that require them to talk.

If you say, 'You know you've been late too often recently,' they can just say 'Yes'. End of discussion, and you've arrived nowhere.

thinking smart

CONFIDENTIALITY

Make sure the person knows that nothing of what is said will go beyond the walls of the office unless they want it to. You won't gossip about them, but they can choose to tell anyone if they want to. None of us like being reprimanded, and if we think that everyone knows about it, it makes it worse. Obviously, if you have to place a note on their personnel file you will make it as objective as possible – outlining only the facts of the incident and what action was taken. Tell them this and make sure they know you keep your word.

Try instead, 'Why have you been late so often recently?' and you might find they open up and explain about their boyfriend borrowing the car to go rallying, which has left it unreliable, and it keeps breaking down, and they have to wait for the AA, who won't come because the car's been modified to unacceptably ferocious standards. You'll be surprised, perhaps, at what answers you do get. The straight, closed questions give you nothing to work with. Open questions give you something to bite on.

'So what happened at the conference?'

'Well, I helped Jimmy carry all the information packs in and hurt my back. I got some painkillers off the receptionist, and then I just had the one gin and tonic at lunchtime and before I knew it I was dancing naked on the table'.

'Ah, and what have you learnt from this?'

'Not to drink at lunchtime?'

'Well, yes, there is that but also not to take any medication from someone you don't know. And perhaps more importantly not to lift things that are too heavy for you. I'll have a word with Jimmy as he knows he's supposed to use that new forklift we bought specifically to stop anyone having to lift anything at conference.'

See, you learned a whole lot more than if you'd just said, 'This is a discipline interview because your

Make sure the person knows that nothing of what is said will go beyond the walls of the office unless they want it to

behaviour was unacceptable last Wednesday. Can't have staff dancing naked on the tables, can we?' 'No'.

You've also found out that bad behaviour can be accidental and unintentional. Once you know this behaviour was not deliberate it can be forgiven much more easily – if you see that as your role. But your lost sheep can also be brought back into the fold much more easily because there is no anger or recrimination – they didn't let you down, they were merely the victim of circumstance.

But what if it had been different?

'So what happened at the conference?'

'Oh, I was so bored. I got a bit pickled in the bar at lunchtime – well, we all like a drink at conference – and then Jimmy dared me to dance on the tables and I just fancied stripping off. Not got a problem with nudity, have you?'

thinking smart

BOOKING THE INTERVIEW

You may well need to book the interview in writing. Drop the person a quick memo saying, 'There's something we need to discuss. I can make Tuesday at 2 o'clock, is that OK for you?' rather than 'I'm holding a discipline interview on Thursday at 10 – be there.' A little tact and diplomacy goes an awfully long way to improving working relations and making the team member feel like that – part of a team.

Now you're in the hotseat. You have an employee who has acted irresponsibly and on purpose. They have admitted their offence but seem quite unabashed by it. They have further compounded their problem by admitting to being drunk – to whatever degree – and they are now challenging you as well. What are you going to do now?

Let's lynch Jimmy

No, don't lynch poor Jimmy for suggesting the dare in the first place. And no, don't rise to the challenge. This interview is about the team member's behaviour, not your views on public nudity or anything else. We'll look in the next

thinking smart

YOU DON'T KNOW HOW THEY FEEL

During the interview there may be a tendency to empathize: 'Look, I know how you feel.' Don't do this. You don't know how they feel. You may think you do, but you don't. At most, you can say, 'I realize you may be feeling pretty bad about this but we need to resolve this problem.' It is best to try and stay away from feelings altogether. You are there to bring a team member back on track. It is a business. You are there to discuss the facts – their actions – and implement ways of correcting their performance. It doesn't have to be an emotional experience at all.

chapter at handling difficult interviews, but it is worth bearing in mind now that you must at all times keep the purpose of the interview uppermost in your mind and not be distracted, nudged off course, irritated, made to feel rotten about having to conduct the interview in the first place, or deflected from your objective. Stay on course, stay calm and stay focused.

So, you've got the person talking and you've got them to admit their actions. Now you must get them to change course. Once they have accepted that their behaviour is unacceptable, you can move on. They may, of course, not see this, so you may have to point out to them how their behaviour affects the rest of the team and how it reflects badly on themselves.

The gap

You expect employees' behaviour to be of a certain standard. Their behaviour has fallen below this. There is a gap. You have to establish that you both acknowledge the same gap – that you are both singing from the same song sheet.

You must both agree what the expected standards of behaviour are. Unless you both agree you will leave the interview with a different set of standards and thus will never be able to reconcile your differences. Suppose you think occasional lateness is fine but frequent lateness is not. They may agree with you. Now define 'occasional' and 'frequent'. It's a bit like the Woody Allen film, where he says, 'We hardly ever have sex – only three or four times a week,' and Annie Hall says, 'We are always having sex – three or four times a week.' They see the gap differently.

For you 'occasional' and 'frequent' may mean once a month is OK but once a week isn't. Your team member may think once a week is fine but

thinking smart

DON'T THREATEN THEM

You are allowed to outline the procedure for repeated offences of this nature: 'If this problem crops up again we shall have to try to resolve it in a different way,' rather than 'You step out of line again and I'm firing you!'

The problem has to be resolved. It has to be resolved in an appropriate way. You are not allowed to threaten the person with actions that are unreasonable or bear no relationship to the offence. You can't threaten to cancel their holidays or take away their company car (unless it is a motoring problem related to the car specifically). Nor can you give them a letter to take home to their parents. This isn't a school; it is a place of business and you are not there to punish them – merely to help them come back on track.

every other day isn't. The key rules for establishing the gap are:

- **outline the expected behaviour**
- **outline where they fall short**
- **define the terms used**
- **agree the gap.**

You must reach a common consensus of the terms used so you both know what the rules are – you must agree what 'occasional' and 'frequent' actually mean in real terms. Once you have done that, you can establish the gap. You may both have a dawning moment when you see the other's point of view: 'Oh, I see why you did this, you thought that dancing on the tables was fine and it was the stripping off that was unacceptable, whereas what I meant was no dancing of any sort.'

A quick example, and then we must really move on. Suppose the discipline interview is about someone taking decisions on matters way above their responsibilities. You establish that they ordered two million extra spare parts for the ZX140 when in fact they have no authority to order anything. They explain that in your absence, they ordered the spares because you said, 'While I'm away, deal with anything that crops up that isn't urgent.'

You didn't specifically tell them not to order anything and they were daft enough not to realize that they shouldn't. You have a gap. Now you've established it, define the terms and set an agenda for an action plan to make sure it doesn't happen again.

FORMALIZING AN ACTION PLAN

Once the employee has admitted that their behaviour is less that what you would have expected and they have appeared suitably contrite – and no, you don't want tears and sobbing, just an acknowledgement that they were wrong – you can move on to the next stage, which is to formalize an action plan.

thinking smart

NO EMOTIONAL BLACKMAIL

Don't be tempted to try emotional blackmail. You know the sort of thing – 'If you foul up you are not just letting yourself down but you are letting me down as well,' and 'I expected better things of you,' or 'Don't you feel ashamed of yourself?'

Stick to the facts and stay on course. Avoid any need to make the person feel more guilty than they already do. This speeds up the interview and stops it becoming difficult. A speedy interview is a good thing, just so long as you both stay calm and agree on all points.

DON'T TALK DOWN TO THEM

You may be senior to the person and more experienced and professional, but avoid talking down to them. Outline the problem. Suggest ways of correcting it and move right along. Don't reminisce, either, about how this happened to you when you were just starting out in their job or whatever. Stay focused on the reason you are both there and get the job done quickly and efficiently – and with the minimum of fuss. Talking down to them, or trying to make them feel small or bad, will only distract you both from the object of the exercise.

This is actually a very simple exercise, but it goes a little beyond the 'I promise I won't do it again' sort of thing. You need to set a formal agenda for positive action. An extracted promise given in the heat of a discipline interview isn't worth the air it's sobbed into. You need a written agreement. But first you must establish the gap.

Setting an action plan

You have to define the terms of what the person should and shouldn't do. Only then can you monitor them to see if they have come up to your standards. It might be as simple as a quick chat in a month's time to make sure they haven't ordered anything in your absence or danced on any tables. Or it might be that they have to check in with you first thing every morning for a week to make sure you know they have arrived on time. Whatever action you jointly decide on – and it must be a joint decision or there is no point to this exercise – make sure you monitor it. If you forget about it, they will think you have no respect for them – they aren't worth the bother. But it also leaves you wide open next time it happens. You have no defence if you have failed to monitor them after a discipline interview.

WRAPPING IT UP

The whole interview should never take more than half an hour. This isn't a long, drawn-out process. You don't need to get heated or angry. You are setting the person straight, not going back over their childhood to see where you went wrong as a parent.

1 Outline the problem – the person's behaviour, actions or performance.
2 Agree the gap between expected standard and actual standards.
3 Formulate an action plan.
4 Wrap it up.

VERBALIZE IN WRITING PLEASE

Obviously you may need to declare this offence as one which warrants a verbal warning. You may also have to log this in writing, but don't make it sound too serious or you risk intimidating the person. If it is a repeat offence, you may need to get a little more serious and declare it sufficiently irksome to warrant a written warning. You must know both your company's policy on these matters and current legislation – don't fall foul of either.

Wrapping it up should take seconds. There is no further business. This isn't an appraisal. There are no other points to be raised. You can't keep the person here and prattle on about their long-term future or even ask them where they think they'll be in five years' time. It is a discipline interview. Even that sounds too harsh and old-fashioned. It is a formal meeting to discuss the person's shortfall in behaviour, actions or performance.

Anyway, whatever it is called, you've done it and now you both need to get out and have coffee. Once you have agreed an action plan, end on a positive note. Don't leave the meeting – or let them leave – on a note of gloom. Lift the air, have

NO BRIBERY

Someone has fallen short of standards. You want them to make up the difference. They too must want to or the interview will lose its way. Don't be tempted to bribe them into good behaviour. No saying, 'Look, you pull your socks up and I'll see about that raise/promotion/new car/redecorated office/a longer lunch break.'

This technique may gain their quick agreement, but you are setting up a lot of long-term problems by doing it. They've effectively got you over a barrel and you will have lost their respect. They must want to come back on track for their own sake. You must be a sufficiently good leader to make them want to follow without having to bribe them.

a laugh, find something positive to say about them so they feel good about the meeting.

Now go away and make a note to yourself to follow up on the action plan, have a coffee, and get on with the rest of your work. Well done. Good job.

You must be a sufficiently good leader to make them want to follow without having to bribe them

Make sure you know and understand you own company's internal discipline procedures, and that you also know and understand any relevant current legislation.

Check out the next chapter about difficult interviews and how to handle them as you won't be able to stop and read it when you suddenly find yourself in the middle of one. Read as much as you can about how to handle difficult people (see *Fast Thinking: Difficult People*). Bear in mind that most discipline interviews need never happen in the first place if the team members are all on your side. This only comes about from good management practices – treat people with respect and they will reward you with improved effort and a desire to never let you down.

Treat people with respect and they will reward you with improved effort and a desire to never let you down

4 handling difficult interviews

Hopefully, if you have taken on board the techniques in the last chapter you won't need anything in this chapter. But life is never quite like that. Difficult interviews crop up from time to time – and you need to be prepared.

Read this chapter if there is the slightest possibility that tomorrow will contain anything unexpected. Yes, that's right, read it anyway as you never know when an interview is going to blow up in your face no matter how diplomatically you've handled it. You are dealing with a human being and they are tricky little beasts.

DIFFERENT TYPES OF DIFFICULT INTERVIEWS

There are various reasons why an interview can be regarded as difficult:

- The team member gets emotional and expresses it as anger or tears.

- It is a follow-up interview to a matter that you thought had been dealt with.

- You've got your facts wrong and are caught on the hop (although if you have followed the advice given in early chapters this shouldn't happen).

- The team member goes all quiet on you and refuses to discuss their actions.

- The team member agrees with everything you say.

- It is a termination interview.

We will look at each of these in turn – and ways to avoid them, of course – but quickly, as we are still thinking at the speed of life and you have a discipline interview tomorrow. I guess you need all the tips you can get if you are to deal successfully with a difficult interview. Let's hope you don't have to.

The emotional team member

Emotional outbursts of any sort are pursuing the same aim – to get you to change direction. If someone cries or shouts it is to get you to stop reprimanding them, sacking them, telling them off, criticizing them – or whatever else you are doing that they don't like. To be blunt, it is a form of blackmail: 'See how you have upset me so much that I am now in tears/really angry?'

In a way, it is a bit like a small child throwing a tantrum. Now, I am not saying that they aren't genuinely upset and feeling emotional but this is a place of business and histrionics are out of place. Any grown-up, responsible person will accept being pulled back into line without crying or getting angry. And, like a small child throwing a tantrum, if you give into it they will do it again … and again … and again. Be firm (not harsh or cruel) and refuse to be swayed by tears or temper tantrums and they should get the message quickly – here is one damn good team leader who is not to be messed with.

thinking smart

IT'S A DISCIPLINE INTERVIEW

The person is there to be reprimanded for a specific offence. They are not there to have their appraisal or a full review of their working life with your company. Stick to the one incident and that alone. This is faster and more efficient unless you want to be there for three hours going over old ground or discussing what happened two years ago at the Christmas party.

If the person becomes emotional, be sympathetic but don't allow it to put you off or change your focus. Follow the five standard rules of discipline interviews:

1 Get the employee to talk.
2 Stick to the facts.
3 Focus on the problem, not the personality.
4 Remain calm yourself and uninvolved emotionally.
5 Be consistent.

Give them time to recover if they get upset but bring them back to the facts. If they become angry, ask them why discussing the facts should be a source of stress – and bring them back to the facts. If they shout at you, remain calm, but remember you do have the right to terminate the interview if you feel threatened. Obviously, you should immediately reschedule it for a later date (and with someone else in attendance) when the person has calmed down. You aren't backing down, merely giving yourself breathing space.

You will find that if you stick to the facts, don't issue ultimatums, and remain calm and businesslike, the chances of you having an emotionally difficult interview are remote indeed.

TISSUE, PLEASE

Always have a discreet box of tissues handy just in case there is any chance of tears – or the person simply needs to blow their nose.

Follow-up interviews to a previous matter

Before you go in, ask yourself why you thought this matter had been dealt with. What more could you have done to prevent it occurring again? Is there some fundamental part of company policy that is flawed and encourages team members to stray off the track? Remember the analogy of the lost lamb? Well, they've got out of the field again. Did you repair the fences last time? Or leave a gap for them to squeeze through? You can't blame a sheep for getting out, it is part of their nature. But you do have to do something about the fences before they do it again.

Then again, you may just have a troublesome sheep. If that's what you've got, you will have to be consider transferring them to another field or changing their responsibilities. Some team members simply don't fit in and will have to be relocated. Some are troublesome because it's in

IN YOUR SHOES

Never begin a disciplinary interview with the phrase, 'And what would you do if you were in my shoes and this had happened?' It will only intimidate them. It is patronizing. They haven't been in your shoes. They don't know what it's like. They don't have your experience. And they may well not have your taste in crocodile lace-ups.

their nature. There is little you can do – you are not their father or counsellor, and you shouldn't take on board that responsibility. Remind them of whatever action plan you formulated last time and look at where it went wrong – together with the person of course. Formulate another action plan and institute more severe ways of monitoring it – yes, I know this means more work for you but it's what you get paid for. Remind them of where their duties lie and what happens if they fail to shape up – this isn't a threat but a timely reminder that ultimately you have to decide whether or not to keep them.

The follow-up interview can be a difficult one. You may need to issue a formal written warning to cover yourself in the eventuality that you decide to

Never begin a disciplinary interview with the phrase, 'And what would you do if you were in my shoes and this had happened?'

terminate their contract – after checking with your higher authorities of course.

You've got your facts wrong

If you are caught out like this – and it does happen, but hopefully not to you after you've read the earlier chapters – then you must terminate the interview immediately and apologize profusely. Don't try and bluff it. Don't try and make out it wasn't your fault. Admit your mistake and move along swiftly.

The team member refuses to discuss their actions

In this case, you should outline the facts and ask open questions to get them talking. If they refuse to do so, just ask an open question and then shut up. The onus is then on them to answer so they'll break before you do. No matter how uncomfortable you find this, remember: they are finding it even more so. Once you've got them talking, you can agree what action you require in the future – and action plans must always be agreed or they just don't work – and let them go. It will all have gone in. They may not be talking but by golly they are listening. You've done your job and stuck to the facts and formulated an action plan. If they aren't playing ball you may need to keep an eye on them for quite a while and find out what the real problem is.

The team member agrees with everything you say

Again, use the same procedure as above – stick to the facts but don't express any opinions – just ask for theirs. Then agree an action plan and move on. This team member thinks they will get away with murder if they just agree with you, so be consistent, treat it like any other discipline interview, and stay focused.

OTHER DIFFICULT INTERVIEWS

The other difficult interview types are:

- **The team member offers to resign – just say you aren't dealing with that issue at this time and stick to the facts.**

- **The team member denies stepping out of line – just make sure you have all the facts in front of you.**

- **The team member always has an excuse – and usually this means passing the buck. Again, stick to the facts and refuse to allow them to incriminate anyone else or blame anyone else. Don't get dragged into debates about details.**

You will meet a lot of others, from the barrack-room lawyer who always knows every point of law, to the 'but we're old mates' team member who doesn't believe you'll reprimand them if they remind you of how you once socialized together and have

No matter how uncomfortable you find this, remember: they are finding it even more so

become blood relatives ever since. There's the out-and-out liar who will invent stories so fabulous you'll be tempted to believe them – don't. Then there's the gossip who, instead of accepting a reprimand, will try to fill you in on all the wrong things others have been doing – don't listen to such busybodying, stick to the facts of this discipline interview. And a hundred more. They're all delightful and should be seen as challenges. Their job is to get you to leave the holes in the fence

WHAT DO THEY TAKE WITH THEM?

The more senior the team member who has to have their contract terminated, the more likely they are to have sensitive information about the company. They will share this information if they leave feeling aggrieved or angry. Make sure they leave feeling you have done them a favour, as they will be much more likely to remain loyal and keep what they know to themselves. Also, if they leave feeling vindictive they can spread false rumours, leak information to the press, blacken your reputation as a team leader, play malicious practical jokes (it does happen), and generally make life difficult for you. The fast-thinking team leader doesn't allow this to happen – they make the leaving team member feel valued and respected even if they have been sacked.

unmended and for them to stray whenever they want. Your job, as humble shepherd, is to bring them back to the flock, mend the fences and keep an eye on them, naughty little lambs that they are.

THE TERMINATION INTERVIEW

This is the one we all hate. But it sometimes has to be done for the good of the team. Now it's your turn to do it and you feel trepidation and anxiety. Of course you do. You are about to make a decision that will deeply affect an individual's life, livelihood and long-term prospects.

The most important thing to remember when facing a termination interview (yep, a sacking) is that your team member has just ceased to be part of a team and now has nothing to lose. They can say what they want, do what they want, and tell you

 thinking smart

LAST THING IN THE DAY

Don't give someone their cards and then expect them to return to their desk as if nothing had happened. If you give someone a week's notice, make it last thing on a Friday. They then have the weekend to compose themselves at least before having to face their workmates.

exactly what they think as well. Let's look at how these three things can be used constructively – or at least how you can defend yourself.

They can say what they want

OK, they can get angry but if you have followed all previous procedures exactly the person will know this is coming. Anger often comes as a reaction to a shock. If you've laid the groundwork well, there will be no shock – and thus no anger. Let them have their say if they need to, though. Your back is broad and you've heard a few choice expletives before so don't get all prissy and defensive. If they need to call you a few names, then so be it.

They can do what they want

Oh no they can't. They can't hit you or destroy the place. Make sure you have someone on standby

thfthithinking smart

SWAP TEAM LEADERS

There is no reason why another team leader can't dismiss or discipline one of your team members instead of you – you may have to repay the favour. Sometimes it removes the heat of the situation if someone slightly more objective and neutral does the disciplining.

whenever carrying out a termination interview just in case. If the person looks as if they might get violent, summon assistance immediately. Do not attempt to restrain someone you've just sacked – it ain't your job and you will only make a bad situation worse.

They can think what they want

… and tell you in no uncertain terms. Good. Let them. Ask them to do so. You will learn a lot about your company from them and about your management style. Let them sound off. Ask them to tell you exactly what they think of the team. You may hear grievances and disputes they've stored up but you may also hear one or two tiny gems that you'd never realized.

thinking smart

TREAT THEM LIKE ROYALTY

Just because someone is having their employment terminated doesn't mean you have to treat them like a pariah. Instead, treat them like royalty. Don't sack them in a corridor or the tiniest cubicle you can find – use a decent office and even treat them to a lunch if they are potentially useful in providing information about where your system has gone wrong. Treat them like royalty, and they will respond accordingly. Treat them as if you don't care about them, and they will be much more difficult.

How to sack people

Hopefully you won't be doing this tomorrow – or in an hour or 15 minutes. But you may have to some day and you need to know the five basic key steps:

- **Present the termination in writing** – this is both a legal requirement and also a useful technique. It avoids the eye-to-eye contact that is so intimidating, and gives the person something to look at while the bad news is digested. They will be grateful for the chance to look away.

- **Stick to the facts** – refuse to discuss anything except totally relevant bits such as termination pay, length of notice, references etc. The person will have known this was coming, so they may have prepared a list of reasons why they shouldn't get the sack, all of which are given to make you feel really bad about it.

- **Use tact and creativity** – don't be belligerent or aggressive, no matter how difficult you find this. Try to find ways to make it easier for both of you. The person may know it is coming and be glad to be gone, so it might not be as desperate as you think.

- **Maintain confidentiality** – if the person doesn't want anyone to know why or when they are going then respect their privacy.

- **Maintain the morale of the team** – let the team know after a termination has been successfully completed why it had to happen. In general terms, you don't have to discuss the specifics of the case and how it affects them. Chances are they will know as much as you do anyway, but they will appreciate being told the facts straight from the horse's mouth.

So there you have it. That's the difficult interview sewn up. Well, it might be if life was as easy as that. But it ain't. People will always think of new ways to fool and fox you, and you will have to stay one jump ahead of the game. You will also have to stay one jump ahead of the legislation if you want to keep your own job. No one higher than you is going to be very tolerant if you discipline team members or even sack them without first following the specific guidelines laid down in both the company procedures and the law. Make sure you know them both well.

SELF-PROTECTION

Here are a few guidelines to enable you to carry out any disciplinary matter without ending up at a disciplinary interview yourself. I know we have

thinking smart

SQUARE PEGS

If you have done your job properly, people who end up being dismissed are invariably what you might term 'difficult'. The fact you have to terminate their employment therefore shouldn't reflect too badly on you, and you should bear in mind that they might well have been a square peg being forced into a round hole. Think of it as an opportunity to liberate them to find their perfect square hole somewhere else.

little time but this lot is important, so take your time and digest them well.

It is a legal requirement for employers to provide written information to all employees about their disciplinary rules and procedures. This should form part of their contract of employment.

The law recognizes the importance of these rules and procedures when it comes to dismissals, and the way the dismissal has been handled will form part of any industrial tribunal's investigation. If the dismissal has been handled unfairly, the employer may well be ordered to reinstate the employee concerned and/or pay them compensation. It doesn't matter if the grounds for dismissal were fair. If the dismissal itself was unfair then you are liable.

thinking smart

BE AVAILABLE

A disciplinary interview can seem terribly intimidating to a team member, especially if they are fairly new. Conduct the interview, but always make sure they know you are available in a less formal setting to discuss any points that the interview may have raised. They may come and see you and have a chat, or they may choose not to, but they will feel reassured that you are available, human and caring. Score extra brownie points.

All procedures and disciplinary procedures have to be seen to be fair by both parties – the employee and the employer – or they won't stand up in an industrial tribunal. They must be reasonable and accepted by both sides.

Any disciplinary rules and procedures must relate to specific incidents and are not to be worded so vaguely as to be meaningless. An industrial tribunal realizes that you can't legislate for every eventuality, but the rules should cover basic safety and maintain satisfactory working relations with all staff.

thinking smart

BRING ALONG A FRIEND

If you give your team member the right to bring along someone else to a disciplinary interview, then you must also have the same rights. If you think the interview is going to get emotional, bring along an assistant or someone from another department or even from personnel and say, 'Oh, this is Ann, she's just going to sit in on this, you don't mind do you?' Invariably they will agree and it diffuses the situation to have a third person there who seems impartial and merely observes, but in reality is there to safeguard your well-being. Obviously, don't bring along someone the person doesn't get on with or who was involved in any previous discipline matter.

Any disciplinary rules and procedures must relate to specific incidents and are not to be worded so vaguely as to be meaningless

Any disciplinary rules and procedures should be part of any new beginner's induction process (see *Fast Thinking: New Beginners*).

Team members should be made aware of what happens to them if they break the rules, and they should be made very aware of what would constitute grounds for a summary dismissal.

Any disciplinary procedures should always follow these guidelines:

- **They should be issued in writing – even if it is a verbal warning.**

- **They must specify to whom they appertain.**

- **They must indicate what disciplinary actions are being taken.**

COUNTING THE COST

If you have to give someone a week's or a month's notice, work out what that costs you financially. Now weigh it up against what it would cost you in lost orders, morale being dragged down, sabotage, poor work performance and the like. If the employee has the potential to damage you financially more by staying, then it sometimes works out cheaper to pay them a week's or a month's wages and let them go early.

- They must be dealt with as quickly as is reasonably possible.

- They must specify which levels of management have what degrees of authority – basically who can sack you and who can't.

- No decisions are to be reached without the team member being informed of the complaints against them.

- Any team member to be disciplined must be given a chance to air their side of things.

- Team members who belong to a union must be given the opportunity to consult their union.

- No team member is to be dismissed for a first offence unless it is a gross violation of company procedures or rules.

- You must provide a right of appeal, and you must tell the team member what that appeal procedure is and how to follow it.

- You must keep records of any disciplinary procedure, even if it is only a verbal warning.

- There must be a reasonable time lapse on offences committed if satisfactory behaviour has been maintained – if a second offence occurs outside this time it is regarded as another first offence.

- It is up to every individual team leader, manager, supervisor, or whatever to keep abreast of current legislation. That means *you*.

It is up to every individual team leader, manager, supervisor, or whatever to keep abreast of current legislation. That means *you*

That should keep you out of court. Remember there is no legal duty to have a disciplinary procedure, but any industrial tribunal is going to look very unfavourably on you if you don't have a pretty good one.

Make sure you have read *Fast Thinking: Difficult People* before you try this at home. Gen up on interview techniques, and ask colleagues what techniques they have found useful. Interview techniques are part of your repertoire as a team leader and you should endeavour to improve all the time. We all make mistakes handing out discipline, but the more you learn the less likely this is to happen.

Make sure you know your company's dismissal procedure extremely well, and that you are up to date with current legislation. Keep records of any disciplinary procedure you have instigated, and make sure any discipline you dish out is backed up with a written record to the team member.

Follow up, follow up, follow up. The three key rules for maintaining good discipline. Be consistent with this, and make sure every team member knows you will be checking to see that if they were late, they are now on time, or whatever. Make notes in your diary to check regularly that minor infringements aren't creeping in and that the team understand's you are fair but firm.

discipline v counselling

I know time is getting on, and you have a discipline interview tomorrow, and you think by now we've covered pretty well everything. But there is a special case to look at – the discipline interview that you suddenly realize should be a counselling interview.

We'll cover this as quickly as possible, but still do it efficiently – thinking at the speed of life. The discipline interview may turn into a counselling interview. If you suddenly decide you are holding the wrong sort of interview, stop what you are doing and rethink your strategy. Obviously you will need to discuss the problem, but you will need to ease off on the discipline and switch hats to a counselling one. Let me give you an example.

Sandra's work has always been good. She's on time and is a very conscientious team member. Of late, however, her work has been of a lower standard. She's misplaced files, burst into tears on more than one occasion, and blown up at quite trivial incidents. And now last Wednesday she stormed out of a meeting and missed another vital deadline. You've pulled her in for a discipline interview although you are sure there is much more to this than meets the eye. On the surface this is a discipline interview, and that is what Sandra is expecting, but you know that you will go easy and try to find out what is going on rather than reprimanding her and sending her on her way – which would undoubtedly exacerbate the situation. Several colleagues have tried asking her what is wrong, but have failed to elicit a response. Now it is down to you as her manager to find the truth.

YOU ARE NOT THE COUNSELLOR

Now let's make one thing very clear – you are not in the business of counselling anyone. It is not your job and you are not trained for it. Even if you are a trained counsellor, it would be unprofessional to counsel someone for a personal problem – or even a work one – if they are directly under you or working as part of your team. What you are going to do is work counselling – finding a way to accommodate someone's personal problems within a working environment.

Back to Sandra. Now you've got her in, what are you going to do? How do you break the ice? Here are the key tips of getting someone to open up and confide in you at a counselling interview:

- Outline the problem as you see it.

- Acknowledge that there might be an underlying problem that you can't see.

- Explain that you are here to help them find a work solution.

- Don't be frightened of silences – don't be tempted to fill them.

- Acknowledge the person's feelings once they do open up.

- Reassure them that their actions are quite normal and that you understand.

- Don't tell them you know how they feel – you don't.

- Ask open questions that require more than a one-word answer.

- Focus your attention on the person and make eye contact.

- Sit in a relaxed posture and make encouraging listening noises – *aha*, *oh*, *ah*, *mmm*.

- After they answer each question, summarize to make sure you fully understand the situation – and that they know you understand.

- Don't offer any judgements or personal opinions – if their partner has left, don't say 'Well, you're better off single, I know I was when I got divorced.'

WHY HELP THEM SOLVE PROBLEMS?
Because if you don't:

- ▶ **your team's productivity will drop**
- ▶ **their morale will fall**
- ▶ **mistakes will be made**
- ▶ **the situation will get worse rather than better.**

You aren't being kind. You are looking after your team's best interests in the best way you know how. Remember that your team member's private life is none of your concern – unless it affects their work. Once it does, it becomes your business. You don't pry into the details, but you do need to take action. The counselling interview is not a 'soft' option, but the wise one.

*ththithi*thinking smart

TENDING YOUR FLOCK
The smart manager watches for signs of any behaviour that is out of place, and corrects it before it has a chance to get worse by suggesting professional counselling and/or offering support. Much as a shepherd will constantly monitor the flock to look for signs of illness or underfeeding or lameness, so too must you tend your flock.

The smart manager watches for signs of any behaviour that is out of place, and corrects it before it has a chance to get worse

Outline the problem

So Sandra comes in and you outline the problem – 'The problem seems to be that your work is going downhill and you are flying off the handle at the slightest thing. Now that's not like you, so can you tell me the reason?'

Now you will find out whether Sandra is just plain bored and looking for another job or, as you thought, has a real problem that is affecting her work.

If Sandra doesn't open up at once – and chances are she won't – you'll need to encourage her. Try saying something along the lines of 'I wonder if there's a problem I don't know about?' or 'If you can give me some idea as to what the problem might be, I might be able to offer some help.'

If you aren't frightened by the silences, sooner or later your team member will open up and start to speak. Perhaps she explains she is very worried about the health of one of her parents and is dreadfully afraid of losing them. Work seems trivial when such a situation occurs, and she gets angry because it all seems so meaningless when someone she loves dearly is in hospital and facing major surgery, for which there is only a slim chance of success.

HELP THEM FIND A SOLUTION

Now you can start to find a solution that will bring Sandra back on track, keep the rest of the team happy, and restore your faith in her work ability. But you do not offer solutions. Oh no. Part of the success of this interview must rest on Sandra suggesting solutions herself. She has to be part of this process to feel helped by it. It is important to get the team member to face up to owning their own problem. Unless they do, any offers of help will seem imposed on them and they might resent it later. They must come up with their own solutions – and you must agree with them, seeing as how you've given them the responsibility. In Sandra's case, it might be to take a couple of weeks off until the crisis has passed.

EXAMINE THE OPTIONS

You need to examine the options before arriving at a solution. Some options will already have been discounted, such as six months' paid leave, or flying Sandra's sick mother to South Africa to recover in the sun, before you arrive at solution time.

If you try to impose a solution from on high, it will backfire. 'Look, I'll give you a couple of weeks off and you can sort this out' will sound like 'I don't want you around while all this is going on.' If the

If you aren't frightened by the silences, sooner or later your team member will open up and start to speak

person comes up with the idea of a couple of weeks off, it is their idea and they have owned their problem.

WHAT TO WATCH OUT FOR

The wise shepherd watches their flock and notices any changes. You too must watch your flock and look out for:

- any falling off in productivity
- deadlines being missed
- bad temper or irritability
- shoddy work
- time wasting
- being quiet or distant
- poor communication
- negative attitude
- lack of enthusiasm
- absenteeism
- lateness
- any uncharacteristic behaviour.

Any one of these on its own may not be important. And any one on its own may be quite normal. What you are looking out for are *changes*. If someone has always turned in good work and suddenly becomes shoddy and turns up late, then you need to look into it.

for next time

Know and understand the real difference between a discipline matter and one that requires counselling. Don't be too ready to suggest professional counselling, though, as some team members may be insulted if they think you think they can't cope.

Know and understand your company's attitude to counselling. Know what systems they have in place and how to effect them. Know who to go to for advice about a counselling matter, and which door to knock on to get impartial advice if you are unsure.

discipline in an hour

Something has happened. Something bad. You've got to move fast. Discipline has to be enforced straight away.

Wrong. A few minutes must be taken first for consideration of all the facts. Do you know:

- who?
- what?
- where?
- when?
- how?
- and most importantly, why?

If you don't know the answer to any of these, then don't go off half cocked. Stop and take the time to find out. An employee's work record may depend on you investigating and finding out. If you fail to do so, you may fail them. You only have an hour, so you must get a move on. Get a sheet of paper and make as many notes as you can.

Get the team member's personnel file and see what their past discipline record has been.

You must know the facts. You must clarify the incident before you can take action. It is better to delay an interview than to go in unprepared. Bear in mind that any discipline interview may come back to haunt you one day at an industrial tribunal.

Remember you have an objective: to establish the truth, to deal appropriately with it, and to make sure it doesn't happen again.

Now you have to:

- Find out the circumstances.
- Give the team member a chance to explain.
- Accept their apology if it is offered in good grace.
- Respect their feelings about the matter and don't give them a hard time.
- Give them a chance to make amends.

That shouldn't take too long. A discipline interview is a serious matter and hopefully you can resolve most disciplinary matters without having to resort to one. If you've simply got to hold one in an hour, then you need to:

- Outline the problem.

- Give the team member a chance to have their say.

- Focus on the incident that led to this interview, rather than be led astray by discussions, such as 'Well, everyone else thought it was a good idea if I absailed down the building.'

- Accept an apology if it is offered.

- Formulate a plan to prevent it happening again, or set in place monitoring systems to make sure you are aware of future behaviour.

- End on a positive note and thank them for coming.

There, that didn't hurt too much. Try to leave more time next time and prepare better. This may have been an easy one but you'd better read the chapter on difficult interviews before you get one.

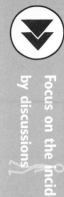

Focus on the incident that led to this interview, rather than be led astray by discussions

discipline in 15 minutes

Don't. That's my advice. There is too much at stake to rush in and risk the repercussions of an industrial tribunal. If you have a discipline interview pencilled in your diary, and you've only just realized, the best you can do is reschedule. If you simply can't do that, at least make sure that:

- ▶ **You know what offence was committed.**
- ▶ **You've got the right person.**
- ▶ **You've got their personnel file in front of you.**
- ▶ **You stick to the facts – and you'd better know them or you'll have to reschedule.**
- ▶ **You give them a chance to explain.**
- ▶ **You jointly agree an action plan to prevent a recurrence.**
- ▶ **You end on a light upbeat positive note.**

That's about the best you can hope for. Next time, leave much more time. This is a serious matter and you need to give your very best to your team members, as you would expect them to give to you. If it is a minor offence, such as being late, then an informal discipline chat (see page 30) might be sufficient, and this you can do in 15 minutes. Give yourself time to be calm and collect your wits. Remain calm and dish out discipline with all the care you can muster. You are the good shepherd and one of your flock has strayed. They don't need punishment, merely guiding back into the field, gently and kindly.